Understanding
CANCER

Understanding
CANCER

by Susan Neiburg Terkel
and Marlene Lupiloff-Brazz

illustrated by Annette Shaw

FRANKLIN WATTS

New York
Chicago
London
Toronto
Sydney

Acknowledgments

The authors would like to acknowledge the following people whose advice and input were appreciated: Gail Barget, Patricia Briggs-Jones, Lenore DeMarsh, Dr. Mitch Fromm, Dr. Lewis Jones, Dr. Craig Gordon, Dr. Marla Rowe Gorosh, Priya Gursaheny, Abby Hrabovsky, Ann Hussar, Emily Lupiloff-Brazz, Molly Lupiloff-Brazz, Jennifer McLaren, Elizabeth Park, Margie Origlio, Stephanie Osmond, Jennifer Russ, Linda Russ, Claudia Tann, Dave Terkel, Jane Turba, Jessica Turba, Harriet Welch, Shawn Wojtowicz, and our editor, Iris Rosoff. We would also like to thank the American Cancer Society and Cancer Family Care, Inc.

Library of Congress Cataloging-in-Publication Data

Terkel, Susan Neiburg.
    Understanding cancer / by Susan Neiburg Terkel and Marlene Lupiloff-Brazz.
       p.   cm.
    Includes bibliographical references and index.
    Summary: An introduction to cancer, its types and treatments, and the common emotions associated with cancer.
    ISBN 0-531-11085-0
    1. Cancer – Juvenile literature.   [1. Cancer.]   I. Lupiloff
-Brazz, Marlene.   II. Title.
RC264.T47   1993
616.994 – dc20   92.38715 CIP AC

To Bernice Massey,
who heals with her heart.
—S.T.

To my children, Emily and Molly,
and my husband, Bill . . . with love.
—M.L.B.

Contents

Cause for CONCERN

Sarah's dad has cancer but Sarah knows very little about the disease. Although her mom tells Sarah that her dad might get cured of cancer, Sarah isn't sure.

If my dad can be cured, Sarah thinks, why does he look so sick, act so tired, and vomit so much after he takes his medicine? And why did he lose all his hair?

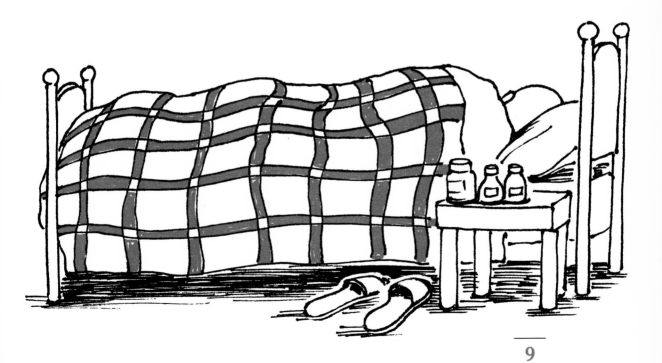

After John's sister got cancer, John was sure it was his fault. Since he had sometimes wished his sister wasn't around to share his toys, John reasoned that now his wish was coming true—and he was terribly sorry. Even so, he was angry, too. For now John's sister seemed to get most of his parents' attention and John was jealous of that.

Like Sarah, when you hear that someone has cancer you may have questions: What is cancer? Why do some people get it? Does it ever go away?

Like John, you may have certain feelings when you think of cancer, such as fear, guilt, anger, frustration, or sadness.

Because there is much that we do not yet know about cancer, we do not know the answers to all our questions. Nor can we avoid all the bad feelings we have when someone we know has cancer. Still, learning about this illness can remove some of its mystery and help us cope better with some of our feelings.

What is CANCER?

Our body is made up of trillions of cells that are so tiny they can only be seen under a microscope. Each cell has a specific job to perform. Red blood cells transport oxygen. Kidney cells help rid the body of waste. Bone cells provide firm support. Nerve cells send messages.

In each cell is a command center, called a *nucleus*. Within this tiny nucleus are thousands and thousands of *genes* that determine everything about the cell.

To replace worn-out cells, certain genes direct the cell to divide into two exact copies of itself. These fresh new copies are called daughter cells. Other genes stop the daughter cells from dividing until they grow old and need to be replaced.

Changes

Occasionally, these "divide-and-stop-dividing" genes, called oncogenes, undergo a change called a mutation.

A mutation in oncogenes can cause a cell to keep dividing, even when the cell doesn't need to replace itself. Furthermore, the mutation causes the new cells to differ from the original cell. In fact, they become so different, we say they are abnormal, which means "not normal."

Abnormal cells can no longer perform the job their original parent cell did—or *any* useful job. Instead, all they do is grow and divide, grow and divide, again and again.

With such uncontrolled growth, abnormal appearance, and uselessness, these cells have become cancer cells.

Too Many Cancer Cells

As more and more cancer cells form, they cluster together into a mass called a solid *tumor*. Because the tumor is made of cancer cells, we say it is *malignant*, which means "harmful."

It takes a lot of dividing before there are enough cancer cells to form a mass large enough to detect. Thus, even small tumors may contain numerous cancer cells. One tumor the size of a marble, for example, contains at least a billion cancer cells. Some tumors grow as large as grapefruits. Imagine how many cancer cells *they* contain!

Normal cells can also grow into a tumor. Indeed, most tumors contain normal cells, not cancer. Tumors that have no cancer are called *benign* tumors, which means "doing little or no harm." Until someone knows *for sure* whether a tumor is benign or malignant, *any* tumor can cause a person to worry.

Solid tumors are not the only form of cancer. When cancer cells occur in fluids or tissue that travel throughout the body, such as blood or *lymph* tissue, they move too much to form a solid mass. Instead, doctors refer to this form of cancer as a *nonsolid* tumor.

You Can't Catch Cancer from Someone Else

Tommy does not want to hug his grandfather because he is afraid of getting his grandfather's cancer.

Tommy *can* hug his grandfather all he wants, though, because cancer is not contagious. It is impossible to catch someone else's cancer by touching him or her. We can hug, kiss, and be close to people with cancer and not worry about getting it.

It is terrible to think that almost any healthy cell can change into a cancer cell, divide again and again, and eventually cause much harm. Isn't it awesome, though, to consider that so many of our cells remain healthy?

WHY?

When Allison's mother and father divorced, Allison blamed her mother for leaving her dad. And she hoped her mother would be punished.

Then her mother got cancer. Allison was afraid. She was afraid that her "bad" thoughts had caused her mother's cancer.

No one's wishes or thoughts can cause anyone's cancer. Still, it is natural to ask: What *does* cause cancer?

Causes of Cancer

In 1945, two nuclear bombs exploded over the cities of Nagasaki and Hiroshima in Japan. These bombs exposed many people there to radiation they would not normally receive. As a result of the damage the radiation caused their genes to suffer, quite a number of those people developed cancer.

No one knows for sure *how* a normal cell becomes a cancer cell. From situations like Nagasaki and Hiroshima, and from others where people have gotten similar cancers, we have learned about some of the leading causes of this disease.

We know that smoking tobacco causes cancer. Indeed, in the United States, smoking is the leading cause of cancer deaths and the second leading cause of all deaths. Nearly six out of seven people with lung cancer smoked, while others with lung cancer have lived or worked with people who smoke.

Substances such as benzene, which is a liquid from coal tar used to make dyes, and asbestos, which was used in the construction of buildings, can cause cancer. Exposure to chemicals like these, especially a great amount of exposure, can cause a person to get cancer.

The ultraviolet rays of the sun can cause skin cancer. Fair-skinned people who sunburn easily increase their chances of skin cancer when they spend too much time in the sun without protection against its harmful rays.

Even some foods may also cause cancer. For example, foods containing certain chemicals used for growing or in preserving may cause cancer. A diet with too much animal fat and too little fiber-containing foods such as fruits and vegetables increases a person's chance of getting cancer.

Anything that tends to cause cancer is called a *carcinogen*. Some products that contain carcinogens, such as cigarettes, are legal and available. On each cigarette package, however, is a warning about cancer. Other substances, such as saccharin, which was used to sweeten food, are no longer available for people to use. In its place, other, supposedly safer, sweeteners are now used.

Good Advice

Despite all we have learned about the causes of cancer, we never know exactly who is going to get cancer and who will be spared. Nor can we predict for sure whose cancer will be cured with treatment and whose will not.

There are nonsmokers who get lung cancer, while some heavy smokers stay cancer-free. Some people in an early stage of cancer fail to be cured, while others in advanced stages are cured. There is so much about cancer and about living and dying that remains a mystery.

Given what we *do* know about the causes of cancer, people can help prevent this disease with this advice:

- Don't smoke, and if you do, quit.

- Protect yourself from the sun's harmful rays.

- Avoid exposure to carcinogens.

- Try to eat healthful food.

Businesses can help prevent cancer, too. For example, tobacco companies can stop growing, selling, and urging people to use tobacco. Companies that make products containing carcinogens can replace them with safer ingredients.

Pointing a finger at smokers and others with cancer and telling them it is their fault does little good. It does nothing to cure their cancer or make them feel better. No doubt they thought they would never get cancer.

On the other hand, why not take the good advice we know about preventing cancer? Some people will still get it, but many more people will not. And that's good news.

ENEMY
Within

It is difficult to imagine our own cells turning against us. But when cancer cells harm the body, then cancer becomes an enemy—an enemy from within.

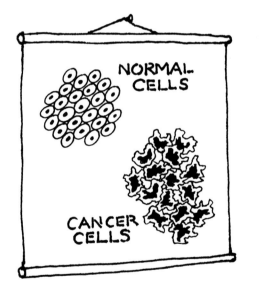

NORMAL CELLS

CANCER CELLS

Laura's dad had *leukemia*, which is a cancer in the tissue of his bones that makes blood cells. This tissue is called bone marrow. As the number of his cancer cells increased, they started crowding out his healthy bone marrow.

In turn, his bone marrow could not make enough red blood cells, which carry oxygen. Without enough oxygen, Laura's dad tired easily.

His cancer cells also overcrowded the stem cells in his bone marrow that produce cells to stop bleeding. As a result, Laura's dad bled and bruised easily.

White blood cells fight off germs. Since his cancerous cells had multiplied faster than his normal ones, Laura's dad now had a lot of white blood cells. In fact, he had *too* many. But cancerous white cells cannot attack germs. Without such protection, Laura's dad was more likely to get infections.

Fortunately for Laura's dad, his leukemia was discovered early and successfully treated. In time, he had plenty of healthy blood cells and no trace of cancerous ones.

Troublemakers

As cancer cells crowd out and destroy healthy tissue and organs, they prevent them from doing their proper work. They also compete with normal cells for vitamins, minerals, and other nutrients the body needs.

Cancer can cause pain, bleeding, and other uncomfortable symptoms. It can interfere with the work the vital organs have to do. Some cancers can even cause death.

On the Move

For some unknown reason, malignant tumors can send out crablike tentacles that invade surrounding healthy tissue or organs. In fact, the word cancer comes from the Latin root meaning "crab."

Another danger of cancer is the ability of cancer cells to break away from their original site and travel anywhere else in the body. There they can start new tumors, called secondary tumors. When cancer has spread and started new tumors, we say it has *metastasized*.

Matt's great-grandpa had cancer in his kidney, the organ that regulates the fluids in our body. Before his tumor was discovered, cancer cells had already spread to his lungs and bones, where new tumors now grew.

This process of breaking away and going elsewhere is one of the biggest dangers facing cancer patients. The more places cancer cells go, the more damage they can do, and the more difficult the cancer becomes to treat.

Cancer cells
growing and spreading

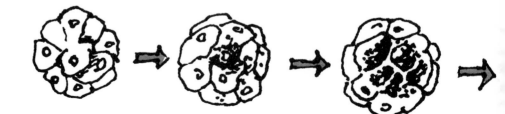

Staging Cancer

When doctors discover a person has cancer, they determine its stage. Which stage they assign a person's cancer depends on

- the size of the cancer and its location

- how much healthy tissue it has invaded

- how fast the cancer is growing

- if the cancer has spread, or metastasized

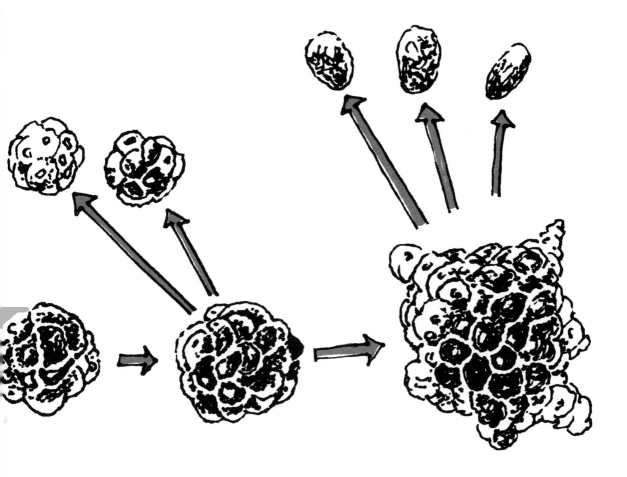

It is better to have a lower than a higher stage of cancer. Ashley's father's cancer was found early while it was a small tumor in his colon and had not invaded any nearby tissue or spread anywhere else. So his cancer was assigned a Stage I.

In contrast, Kevin's neighbor's bone cancer was not *diagnosed* until it had already spread to his lungs and his liver, where secondary tumors were now growing. As a result, his cancer was assigned a Stage IV, which is far more difficult to cure.

●

Our cells, tissues, and organs are working all the time, day and night, to keep us alive. Anything that interferes with their work, especially the vital work of lungs, brain, blood, kidneys, or liver, means trouble. And cancer can cause that trouble, especially in an advanced stage.

5

Kinds of CANCER

There are actually over one hundred different kinds of cancers, depending on what kind of cell is involved and where the cancer begins in the body.

For example, cancer that *starts* from a lung cell is lung cancer. If breast cancer cells go to the lung and form tumors there, those new, secondary tumors are breast cancer, not lung cancer. Likewise, the lung cancer cells that spread to the liver are not liver cancer; they remain lung cancer.

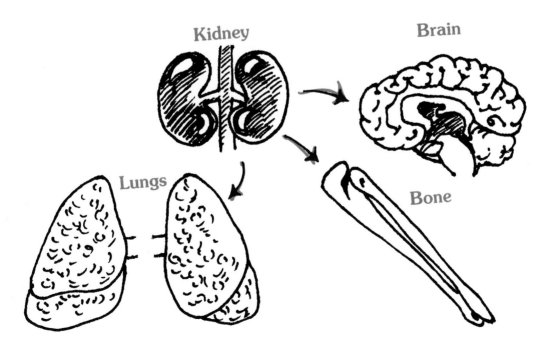

Kidney   Brain

Lungs

Bone

This might be easier to understand if you imagine being born and raised in Texas, moving to Italy, and still calling yourself a Texan!

There are many places in the body where cancer can begin. Only organs like the heart, whose cells never divide or replace themselves, cannot begin a cancer growth.

●

Some cancers, like skin cancer, are common. Each year in North America, for example, over half a million skin cancers are treated. Other cancers, like cancer of the nose or gallbladder, are rare. Each year such cancers are found in only a few hundred people.

The most common cancers start in the

- skin
- lungs
- colon or rectum
- breast (in women)
- prostate
- pancreas
- blood
- ovary

Who Gets Cancer?

Anyone at any age can get cancer. Nevertheless, cancer is *much* more likely to occur in older people, especially those over sixty-five years old.

One out of every 3 adults will have cancer sometime in his or her life. In sharp contrast, cancer strikes only 1 out of every 10,000 children.

Cancer is also more likely to occur in people exposed to carcinogens. For example, smokers or tobacco chewers are more likely to get cancer than people who don't smoke or chew tobacco.

Kimberly's grandmother died from ovarian cancer. (An ovary is a female sex gland.) Now Kimberly's aunt has it. Kimberly is concerned that when she grows up, she will get ovarian cancer, too.

Just as in Kimberly's family, certain cancers, such as breast or ovarian cancer, can run in families. This family link is referred to as a genetic factor.

But being "more likely" to get a certain cancer in a family does not mean that *each* person in the family will get it. Those family members like Kimberly, who are at risk, though, need to be on the lookout for the kind of cancer that does appear to run in their family.

Cancer has a nasty reputation for making many people very sick. However, most people, especially when they are young, are *never* going to get cancer. Many people who do get cancer will probably get cured. And certainly, everyone should try to avoid the causes of cancer and maintain a healthy life-style.

6

Finding CANCER

There are many ways to diagnose, or find, cancer. Some people discover cancer when they see or feel a change in their bodies.

Most moles are harmless. But Jennifer's aunt had a mole on her face that became discolored and grew. This

change prompted her to see her doctor, who sent a sample—called a *biopsy* specimen—of the mole to a special laboratory called *pathology*. Cancer cells were found in the specimen, and the mole was removed.

Cancer Screening

At their regular medical examinations, many grown-ups undergo routine tests to check for cancer. Such tests are called screening tests.

Different screening tests find different cancers. Mammograms are X-ray pictures of the breast that screen for breast cancer. In another type of test, doctors use a hollow tube with a light at the end to look inside a person's colon for any growths that might be cancerous.

Other cancer-screening tests include taking samples of blood, stool, urine, and other bodily fluids and checking the samples for evidence of cancer.

Because cancer occurs so rarely in young people, they are normally not screened for it. Instead, cancer screening usually begins when a person is older and the chance of having cancer has increased.

People with a family history of cancer or exposure to cancer-causing substances are also routinely screened for certain cancers.

During her pregnancy, Shana's grandmother had taken a powerful drug, DES, that her doctor thought would keep her from losing her baby. Years later, she learned that DES can cause cancer in the daughters of women who had taken it. Knowing that she has an increased chance of getting cancer now, Shana's mother is screened for it every six months.

The Warning Signs

As cancer grows, it can cause symptoms that warn a person of its presence. The following is a list of the most common warning signs of cancer:

- sores that don't heal
- changes in a mole or wart
- new lumps and bumps
- coughing or hoarseness that does not go away
- unusual bleeding, such as blood in the urine or stool
- pain that doesn't go away
- fever that doesn't go away
- unexplained weakness, weight loss, or a tired feeling

Any of these symptoms may be due to a medical problem that is not cancer. A persistent cough, for example, may be a sign of a chest infection. Headaches, fevers, and exhaustion may all be symptoms of other medical conditions.

Making Sure

To find out if a person's warning sign is cancer or not, doctors do a variety of tests.

One morning in the shower, Bill's mother felt a lump in her breast. She was concerned that the lump might be cancerous.

First, Dr. Anderson looked at a mammogram of her breasts. On the film he saw a suspicious mass. But he was still unsure if the lump was malignant or benign. He needed to do more tests.

After giving Bill's mother some painkilling medicine, Dr. Anderson tried to withdraw some fluid from the lump with a needle. (If there had been any clear fluid, he would have thought the lump was probably harmless.)

No fluid came out.

The next thing Dr. Anderson did was remove the lump at a hospital and send it to the pathology lab for a biopsy. There, the sample of tissue was stained with a special dye and viewed under the microscope. (Dye makes cancer cells more noticeable.)

No cancer cells showed up. When Dr. Anderson informed Bill's mother that she did not have cancer, she was happy and relieved.

●

Another way to confirm cancer is by a test called a CAT *scan*. With it, a doctor can detect a tumor as small as a pea. Other kinds of machines can detect even smaller tumors than this.

Besides these ways, doctors have still other tests to

diagnose cancer. For instance, they can measure special chemicals in the blood. Or they can trace radioactive substances through the body.

Hide and Seek

Not all cancers show up in screening tests or give early warning signs. Sometimes cancer remains undetected until it has become quite advanced. Or it is found accidentally when doctors are dealing with other medical problems.

As new tests are developed and as more people take advantage of the screening tests we already have, more cancers will be detected earlier when the chances for cure are greater.

●

Everyone wants a clean bill of health. Sometimes the fear that cancer may be lurking keeps people from wanting to look for it, even with a warning sign. Perhaps as people learn that the key to cancer treatment is to find it before it spreads too far or does too much harm, they will have tests for cancer as early as possible.

7

Treating CANCER

Jessica went to the hospital to visit her grandfather, who was being treated for cancer. When Jessica saw Grandpa Bonner, she was surprised to see how he looked—not at all like his usual self.

Lying in a hospital bed, Grandpa Bonner had tubes in both his arms, tubes in his nose, and a sad look on his face. His lips were chapped and he didn't feel much like talking. And the odor in his room was not at all like the musty smell of pipe tobacco and hickory wood that always surrounded Grandpa Bonner.

Without treatment, Grandpa Bonner would eventually be too sick to survive his cancer. Left alone, cancer continues to grow and spread. Even with treatment, Grandpa Bonner may not recover.

⬤

The treatment for cancer varies. For some patients, treatment is painless and easy. For others, it can mean many operations, taking a lot of medicine and other treatment, and frequent hospital stays with long periods of sickness.

A doctor who specializes in treating cancer, an *oncologist*, selects a treatment plan for each patient. This plan is called a protocol and depends largely on the kind of cancer the doctor is treating and how early or advanced it is.

Many cancer treatments are effective, especially if they are given at an early stage of the disease. When treatment works so well that no trace of cancer is found anymore, we say the patient is in *remission*. And we celebrate his or her good news.

Patients who remain in remission, or free of cancer, for a certain number of years—usually five—are considered cured. Today, half of all cancer patients can look forward to being cured.

Removing the Tumor

One way to treat cancer is to remove it. Skin cancers can usually be removed in the doctor's office. Larger tumors, or those deep inside the body, however, must be removed in a hospital or clinic.

During recovery, many patients need more rest than usual and help with the work they usually do. This may mean that someone else may be cooking for you, putting you to bed, and taking you to your lessons or activities.

When a tumor is removed, healthy tissue may be removed as well. Sometimes, it is even necessary to remove an entire organ or limb. This is to make sure that any cancer cells that might have invaded the surrounding tissue are not left behind to grow and spread.

Doctors found cancer in Chloe's grandmother's kidney and removed the kidney. To treat the cancer in Paul's hip, his hipbone was removed and replaced with an artificial one.

Chloe's grandmother was sorry to lose her kidney, and Paul was sorry to lose his hipbone. However, both were relieved to get rid of their cancer.

Zap It

Another common way to treat cancer is with *radiation therapy*. Beams of radiation emitted from a machine destroy a cancer cell's ability to divide. As a result, the cancer cells stop dividing and eventually die. As more and more of the cells die, the tumor shrinks or disappears altogether.

Unfortunately, some of the radiation also reaches healthy cells and damages them, too. For this reason, the patient does not receive all the radiation treatment at one time. Rather, it is usually spread out over a period of time.

To shrink his malignant tumor, Katie's stepfather drove to the hospital for radiation therapy every Monday through Friday for six weeks. Having the weekends off allowed his healthy cells some time to recover from the effects of the *irradiation*.

Instead of coming from machines, radiations are sometimes emitted from rods called implants. The doctor skillfully positions these rods near the cancer. Then they are left in place for a few days so they can continually emit tiny doses of radiations that destroy the cancer.

And the Medicine Goes Down

As we have learned, nonsolid tumors like leukemia (cancer of the blood) are constantly on the move. We also learned that cancer can metastasize and start secondary tumors. To treat such conditions, oncologists rely on a treatment called *chemotherapy*.

Here, cancer patients are given anticancer drugs capable of destroying cancer cells anywhere in the body, including those cells missed by surgery or irradiation.

Like radiation therapy, chemotherapy destroys healthy cells at the same time it is trying to destroy cancer cells. Therefore, oncologists must be careful not to give more anticancer drugs than a patient's body can safely handle.

Anticancer drugs may be taken as pills or injections. Or they may be mixed in a liquid that slowly drips into the patient's vein. This procedure is called an *IV*, which stands for intravenous (meaning "in the vein").

Side Effects

Radiation and anticancer drugs can cause terrible side effects. These include hair loss, mouth sores, sore throats, and feeling sick to the stomach. Many people suffer from diarrhea, lose weight, feel tired and achy, and long to finish their treatment course. Sometimes they even feel as though the treatment is making them sicker than their cancer.

Most of these side effects go away once treatment is over. Hair grows back, the appetite returns, and life often returns to normal.

Other Treatment

Besides surgery, radiation therapy, and chemotherapy, doctors have still other ways to treat cancer. Some of these include transplanting healthy bone marrow into cancer patients, or using *monoclonal antibodies* that help the patient's own immune system destroy the cancer.

Eager to find a cure for their cancer, some people turn to other treatments that are still experimental and of unproven safety or effectiveness. These treatments include new anticancer drugs, special diets, and laetrile (a substance taken from apricot pits).

Even though they cannot cure cancer, there are also treatments to make cancer patients feel better, such as painkillers and surgery to reconstruct body parts lost to the disease.

●

One reason many people dread having cancer is because to get better they may have to endure treatment that makes them feel terrible. Or they may have a cancer that cannot be controlled with treatment.

Nevertheless, doctors have many effective ways to treat people with cancer. Some have been discovered only recently, such as a new treatment for ovarian cancer that comes from scruffy yew trees growing in our forests. Many of these treatments offer hope—and even health—to cancer patients.

When the Going Gets ROUGH

8

It is hard to watch a person you love and care about have cancer.

Dan's mother has had cancer for four years now. It is quite advanced. Much of his mother's time is spent in treatment or recovering from the effects of treatment.

Some days his mother feels strong enough to help Dan with his homework or play a game of checkers with him. Most of the time, though, she is too tired and sick to do almost anything.

With mounting medical bills to pay, Dan's father works an extra job now. Family and friends try to help out by making meals and taking Dan and his sister to school and other activities. Dan has taken on more responsibilities, from preparing simple meals to helping with the laundry and housecleaning.

With all these changes and added duties, Dan sometimes feels cheated and unhappy. He longs to have his mother's cancer disappear and have her well again. And he worries about whether that is ever going to happen.

Tough Times

Not all people struggle with cancer as much as Dan's mother and her family. For the many who get cured, health returns and life continues much as it was before. But as Dan and his family have learned, cancer can bring tough times—some very tough times.

Having a family member sick with cancer can be embarrassing or hard to explain. Watching a brother or sister with cancer get extra attention can make you feel jealous or left out.

Like Dan, you may be asked to do extra chores around the house. You may not always welcome having other people in your house helping out. At times, you may feel lonely. If everyone is busy taking care of the sick person in the family, you may feel that they are not taking as much care of you as you deserve.

People with cancer may talk about dying. Sometimes they don't do this, but you worry about their dying anyway. Or their cancer appears to go away, but everyone worries about it coming back.

Dealing with Cancer

For many people, having cancer makes life seem more valuable. Each day feels like a gift. But with so much to worry about, dealing with cancer can also bring stress and despair.

During such ordeals, many people become gentle warriors and find courage, grace, wisdom, and humor to help them through. But even the bravest, most cheerful people get down at times. Remember, nobody is perfect and no one has to be.

It is normal to cry. It is normal not to be able to cry, too. It is normal to get angry. And it is normal to be sad and depressed.

When someone you know has cancer, it can help to talk about your thoughts and feelings with someone else. If you cannot discuss this with your parents, you might find a relative, family friend, teacher, or counselor whom you trust. Some children find it helpful to pray, to write letters or poems, or even to talk to their pets or toys.

●

Cancer doesn't just affect the person who has it. Family and friends are affected as well. By coping with cancer as a team, everyone can share the hardship that this illness brings. Indeed, it is the sharing and caring together that give us strength to overcome the tough times.

Looking On the BRIGHT Side

9

When Jordan's uncle found out he had cancer, everyone in the family cried. They loved Uncle Charlie and knew he had a serious disease.

For nearly a year, Uncle Charlie underwent treatment. He lost his hair. He vomited up Thanksgiving dinner. And he was so tired, that he slept through the fireworks on the Fourth of July.

That was a few years ago. Today, Uncle Charlie is free of any trace of cancer. And chances are that he'll remain in remission long enough to be considered cured.

Not every cancer story has a happy outcome. But researchers around the world are looking for—and finding—new ways to treat cancer so that more and more people like Uncle Charlie can survive.

Someday, perhaps, we will find a cure for every cancer, or a way to prevent it altogether. And we all hope that time comes soon.

Glossary

benign tumor: a noncancerous tumor

biopsy: removing a sample of tissue for viewing under a microscope

cancer: uncontrolled growth of abnormal cells

carcinogen: any substance or agent that produces cancer

chemotherapy: treatment of cancer with chemical substances

diagnosis: confirmation that cancer is present or not

genes: proteins in cells that determine everything about the cell

irradiation: the application of radiations in the treatment of patients

IV: a tube that allows liquid to be dripped directly into a vein

leukemia: cancer that is found in bone marrow

lymph system: network that circulates fluid to bathe each cell; produces and stores cells that fight off germs and infections

malignant tumor: a cancerous tumor

mastectomy: removal of the breast

metastasis: spread of cancer from original site to somewhere else in the body

monoclonal antibodies: through genetic engineering, antibodies are produced to respond to specific tumor cell lines

nucleus, nuclei: part of the cell that contains the genes

oncologist: a doctor who treats cancer

pathology: the study of disease; pathology lab is where diseased tissue and its causes are examined

prognosis: medical outlook for the future of a cancer patient

radiation therapy: use of X rays to treat cancer

radiations: beams of X rays

remission: free of any evidence of cancer

reoccur: when cancer returns

scan: test using radioactive substance to locate tumors

tumor: an abnormal mass of tissue

For Further Reading

Fine, Judy Laine. *Afraid to Ask.* New York: Lothrop, Lee & Shepard, 1978.

Fradin, Dennis. *Cancer, A New True Book.* Chicago: Childrens Press, 1988.

LeShan, Eda. *When a Parent Is Very Sick.* Boston: Atlantic Monthly Press, 1986.

Silverstein, Alvin, and Virginia B. Silverstein. *Cancer: Can It Be Stopped?* New York: J.B. Lippincott, 1987.

For More Information

To get free pamphlets, call the American Cancer Society Hotline: 1-800-227-2345, or 1-800-4-CANCER

Your public library may also have pamphlets about cancer.

Index

About the Authors

Susan Neiberg Terkel grew up in Lansdale, Pennsylvania, and was educated at Cornell University, where she studied child development and family relationships. She is the author of several books for young people, including *Understanding Child Custody*, *Should Drugs Be Legalized?*, and *Abortion: Facing the Issues*. Ms. Terkel lives in northeast Ohio with her husband and three children.

Marlene K. Lupiloff-Brazz is a writer, counselor, and community educator, who has made women's and children's issues the focus of her work. As a cancer survivor herself, Ms. Lupiloff-Brazz co-authored this book in response to the needs of both her own children and the children of cancer patients everywhere. Ms. Lupiloff-Brazz lives in Michigan with her husband, two daughters, and four pets.

10-96

DATE			